American pop culture

FaSHion

Ursula Rivera

Children's Press®
A Division of Scholastic Inc.
New York / Toronto / London / Auckland / Sydney
Mexico City / New Delhi / Hong Kong
Danbury, Connecticut

Book Design: Michael DeLisio and Mindy Liu
Contributing Editor: Shira Laskin
Photo Credits: Cover © Jeff Greenberg/Index Stock Imagery, Inc.; p. 4 © Pace
Gregory/Corbis Sygma; p. 7 © Louis K. Meisel Gallery/Corbis; pp. 8, 10, 13, 16, 33
© Bettman/Corbis; p. 15 © Peter Hince/Getty Images; p. 18 © Rolf Bruderer;
p. 21 © Henry Diltz/Corbis; p. 23 © AP/Wide World Photos; pp. 26, 32, 36
© Reuters NewMedia Inc./Corbis; p. 29 © Corbis; p. 30 © AFP/Corbis; p. 31
© Rune Hellestad/Corbis; p. 35 © Neal Preston/Corbis; p. 40 © Roger Ball/Corbis

Library of Congress Cataloging-in-Publication Data

Rivera, Ursula.
    Fashion / Ursula Rivera.
    p. cm.—(American pop culture)
    Published simultaneously in Canada.
    Includes bibliographical references and index.
    ISBN 0-516-24072-2 (lib. bdg.) ISBN 0-516-25945-8 (pbk.)
    Early days of design—Dress of the decades—Popular culture—A
    fashionable future.
    1. Fashion—Social aspects—United States. 2. Fashion—United
States—History. 3. Clothing and dress—Social aspects—United States.
I. Title. II. Series.

GT605.R58 2004
391'.00973—dc21
                                        2003009155

1 2 3 4 5 6 7 8 9 10 R 13 12 11 10 09 08 07 06 05 04

Contents

When celebrities, such as Halle Berry, are in the spotlight, they depend on top designers for the perfect look.

Introduction

A long, black limousine pulls up to the red carpet for an awards show. The door opens and out steps a famous Hollywood star. Photographers surround her with clicking cameras and flashing lights.

The star is stunning as she stops to have her picture taken. She turns slightly so people can see the glamorous details on the back of her dress. Everyone oohs and ahs over the beautiful design. There is only one question on their minds: *Who is she wearing?*

Someone calls out the question and the star answers by naming a designer. The crowd smiles and nods—the dress is truly a work of art. As other stars arrive, many designers' names are heard. There are shouts of Calvin Klein, Richard Tyler, and Donna Karan.

Then there are more of Marc Jacobs, Helmut Lang, and Ralph Lauren. The level of excitement rises as the names are called. Who are these designers—and why are their names so important?

The answer is *fashion*. Fashion has a very special place in American popular culture. Fashion is celebrated because of its ability to demonstrate what is extraordinary about America. American designers left behind European style traditions to create unique American looks. What they have produced over the years are expressions of America's fun-loving, casual spirit.

American fashion does more than cover bodies. It celebrates the emotions, mood, and thoughts of Americans throughout the country's history. Designs reflect America's ever-changing culture. As different events take place, and ways of thinking change, so do fashion designs. As these designs develop, they take their place in popular culture.

Fashion boldly reflects what it is to be American at any given time. Designs are clear,

Window displays of new fashions are often works of art, inspiring shoppers to buy what's inside.

loud statements that capture in color and fabric what cannot be put into words. America's fashion is Jennifer Aniston's haircut during the first season of *Friends*. It is also the revealing dress Jennifer Lopez wore to the Grammys in 2000. Fashion is the uniform nurses wear at the hospital and the design of a blazer worn by an airline pilot. In all its many forms, fashion is one of the most exciting pieces of American popular culture!

When early settlers brought European styles with them to America, they didn't count on the hard work it would take to build communities. Imagine working outdoors in this fancy seventeenth-century footwear!

Early Days of Design

Early American Fashions

Environment played a large role in early American designs. When people traveled to America in the seventeenth century, they brought stylish European clothing with them. This clothing was designed to look beautiful and sophisticated. However, people soon realized that these fashions were not durable enough for life in the New World. Early Americans spent much of their time working outdoors to build houses and communities. They needed clothing that would last through their tough work. Heavy wool and canvas

Looking good didn't always *feel* good. To achieve the popular hourglass look, women had to lace up their middles as tightly as possible.

replaced the stylish, yet delicate, materials used by European designers.

As American cities developed and grew, fashion took on a different role. Life was no longer about survival. It had become a little easier for most people. Designers took this opportunity to bring more decorative fashions back into style. They were able to use lighter fabrics such as velvet, silk, and linen. Lace and embroidery appeared in tasteful patterns on cuffs and collars.

European Styles

Throughout the eighteenth and nineteenth centuries, the royal courts of Europe inspired American fashion. Since America was still a very young country, it was often influenced by older nations. During this time, designed clothing was only for the richest people in American society. Wealthy men and women wore elegant clothing. Suits and gowns involved many layers of fabric, creating a formal look for the upper class.

By the mid-1800s fashionable women's dresses took on the shape of an hourglass. A well-dressed woman's profile was now wide and circular at the bottom, as narrow as possible at the waist, and wide again toward the shoulders. Women wore corsets and petticoats underneath their clothing to create this look. Corsets were body wraps that laced and tied across a woman's back to pull her waist inward. Petticoats were layers of fabric worn under a skirt to fluff it out. Both items made it difficult for a woman to move around.

This carried out the idea that a woman's role was as a decorative object. Styles changed only slightly leading up to the twentieth century. The 1900s, however, brought many exciting new designs.

Flappers to Zippers

During the 1920s there were great changes made in women's fashion. American women were slowly starting to break away from traditional roles. Many women became more independent, working and living on their own. Some of these women began to wear makeup and go out without chaperones. They became known as flappers. Designers honored this freedom with a completely new style. Dress designs were looser and the waist was no longer squeezed in. Corsets were no longer worn and skirt lengths rose to just below the knee. Although these fashions were expensive, they were popular.

Life in the United States changed during the hard economic times of the 1930s. Many people lost their jobs and life savings. In the

Flapper fashions of the 1920s gave women the freedom to cut loose on the dance floor.

years that followed, Americans had much less money to spend on clothes. Expensive fashions were no longer an option. People wanted to buy well-made items that would last. Designers had to make changes based on the more careful approach to spending during the 1930s. One of these changes was to try to lower the cost of clothes. The zipper was introduced and became the favorite way to close anything from jackets to pants. It cost less than buttons to make, so prices dropped.

Wartime Changes

During the 1940s America was involved in World War II. Most men were fighting in Europe, so women took their places in the workforce. Clothing trends began to change. During the war, it was expected for women to wear pants. They would have had trouble doing work in dresses or skirts. When the war ended, American men returned to their jobs, and many women returned to their lives as homemakers. Designers gave women's fashion a makeover. The "New Look" was introduced, with long flowing skirts, the return of tight waistlines, and other feminine details. This style encouraged the idea of women as decorative objects once again.

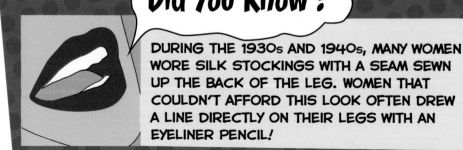

Did You Know?

DURING THE 1930s AND 1940s, MANY WOMEN WORE SILK STOCKINGS WITH A SEAM SEWN UP THE BACK OF THE LEG. WOMEN THAT COULDN'T AFFORD THIS LOOK OFTEN DREW A LINE DIRECTLY ON THEIR LEGS WITH AN EYELINER PENCIL!

The poodle skirt fad ended as quickly as it began—but not before helping to define a decade.

Keeping up the feminine styles, the 1950s was the era of poodle skirts. These felt skirts, a favorite with teenage girls, originally included a sewn-on patch in the design of a poodle. Other patches became popular, including flowers, records, and cars. However, America was changing and poodle skirts didn't last long. In the years that followed, styles would change rapidly.

With their denim pants, white shirts, and ponytails, young women of the 1950s boldly set themselves apart from their parents' generation.

Dress of the Decades

Since the middle of the twentieth century, American fashion trends have grown and changed quickly. Each decade brought new and exciting designs that reflected the spirit of America.

Denim Nation

In the 1950s and early 1960s, denim became an American icon. What began as work clothing was transformed into the core of American fashion. During this time period, the denim craze started—and hasn't stopped.

No one could have guessed that miners' work clothes from the 1850s would take over American fashion—and unite a country in denim for years to come.

In the 1850s Morris Levi Strauss began a company in San Francisco that manufactured rugged denim pants for coal and gold miners. By the mid-twentieth century, all kinds of Americans had adopted the "Levi's" look. Denim was comfortable and cheap because it was made in America.

The pants also had a unique ability to make all people who wore them equal. When a person put on a pair of jeans, his or her clothing no longer announced salary, age, or gender.

He could easily be a part of the working class, or even the president of the United States. Denim's casual style connected the many different people that make up America, freeing them from being labeled. It was a look that truly captured America's personality.

The Rise of Ready-to-Wear

In the 1950s and 1960s, it was also common for women to sew clothing for themselves. At this time, however, many American women also began to take jobs outside of their homes. With families to take care of, and new work responsibilities, women had little time to make clothes. Clothing companies and designers got together and came up with a solution: ready-to-wear clothes for women.

Ready-to-wear clothes are designed in a number of standard sizes and made in factories. Until this time only men's clothing was sold this way. American men's fashions were simple, and changed little. They were easy to produce in large quantities. For women's styles, however, this was a brand-new idea. Now women could walk into a store, select clothing in the perfect size, and buy it on the spot.

Ready-to-wear clothing was good for American business. It provided companies with a good way to sell clothes to many women. Manufacturers saved money by buying fabric in huge batches. They then produced a massive number of identical items that were distributed to stores all over the country. Ready-to-wear also encouraged the sale of clothing lines. A clothing line is a series of designs, such as shirts, dresses, or skirts that have certain elements of style in common. Clothing lines increased competition between department stores as they began to offer women different price ranges and styles.

Flower Power

There were radical changes in America during the late 1960s and 1970s. The peace-loving hippie movement brought both wild patterns and a flowing style to fashion. Many young

As hippies spread peace and love across America, designers spread the width of sleeves and the playfulness of paisley to American youth.

people of this era lived their lives differently from their parents. They protested against United States participation in the Vietnam War, hoping for people to live together in harmony. There was a huge rise in awareness about equal rights, health, and the environment.

The younger generation believed in peace and acceptance. Tie-dyed shirts and skirts captured this feeling and became wildly popular. Their many colors swirled together reflected the idea of America as a melting pot of many cultures.

During this time, men's fashion finally turned away from mass-produced suits. Brightly colored fabrics, polyester, bell-bottom pants, and turtlenecks replaced more conservative looks. Ties grew wider at the bottom— sometimes as much as five inches across— and were often covered in bold patterns such as stripes and paisley. It was a very colorful time in American fashion.

Land of the Brand

Brand names tagged the fashion world in the 1980s and 1990s. A brand name is the name of the maker of a product. It also represents that product's quality. For example, Americans knew that brand names such as Ford and Chevrolet stood for quality American craftsmanship. In fashion, brands also expressed a particular style. Gradually, brand names in clothing became as important as they were in other industries.

High-end designers, such as Calvin Klein and Donna Karan, became famous for their

A designer's job is never done. Here is Donna Karan, busy with models backstage before her DKNY show in February 2003.

trendy, modern styles. Their names became *very* well known in American fashion. In fact, designers sold the right to use their names to other companies. The companies would use the brand names to sell their own products. For example, a company could buy the *Donna Karan* brand name to place on a line of sunglasses they manufactured. Since people knew that name, and what it represented, they trusted that the sunglasses were worth buying.

Both the sunglasses company and Donna Karan's company made money from the deal. This process is called licensing and is successful today.

Lower-end retail stores such as Kmart and Wal-Mart began looking for celebrities to create brand names for less-expensive fashions. Linking products with familiar faces proved successful. Branded collections became big business. TV stars and former fashion models began designing collections of their own, including Jaclyn Smith, Cheryl Tiegs, and Kathie Lee Gifford.

A Casual Close to the Century

There were many popular styles at the end of the twentieth century. Each one stayed true to the American spirit of casual comfort. Youth trends played a big part in the fashion marketplace. Boys' jeans grew bigger and baggier, and were worn low on the hips. American girls fell in love with bell-bottoms and peasant tops that looked like those their parents wore in the 1970s.

Fashion in the workplace took an interesting turn as dress-down Fridays became popular. This allowed business people to wear casual clothing, such as jeans, to the office on Fridays. The idea pushed the entire country toward a more casual work environment. Instead of always wearing suits to the office, some people had the option of a more relaxed look.

These fashion trends are celebrations of moments in American popular culture. They give us a glimpse into what America considers important, beautiful, or comfortable in different times. Many of these trends were the brilliant ideas of creative designers. Others emerged out of the celebrity spotlight.

Did You Know ?

FASHION MADE ITS WAY INTO THE FAST-FOOD INDUSTRY IN THE 1990s. DURING THAT DECADE, FAST-FOOD COMPANIES SPENT OVER $6 BILLION ON SPECIALLY DESIGNED UNIFORMS FOR THEIR EMPLOYEES.

For more than two decades, the Material Girl, Madonna, has been a symbol of popular fashion in America.

Popular
Culture

People in the spotlight often inspire fashion trends. Celebrities carefully choose what they wear while in the public eye. People watch them, enjoy how they look, and want to imitate their style.

Fashion and Hollywood

Costume design is the art of selecting and creating the clothing actors wear on-screen. It has always been an important part of the most popular movies and TV shows. Clothing can say so much about the person wearing it, so costumes help audiences understand characters. As people in the audience relate to these characters, these costumes can inspire fashion trends.

One of the most famous movie-inspired fashion trends happened in 1961. Audrey Hepburn starred in the movie *Breakfast at Tiffany's,* wearing a simple black evening dress and dark sunglasses. She looked elegant and sophisticated. Many American women wanted to be just like her. Hepburn's appearance in the movie created a demand for outfits identical to those she wore. Even today, a simple black dress remains a classic evening outfit, and dark glasses are considered glamorous.

In 1977, the film *Annie Hall,* directed by Woody Allen, was released. The main female character, played by Diane Keaton, wore men's suits, ties, and hats in the movie. This sparked another trend with American women.

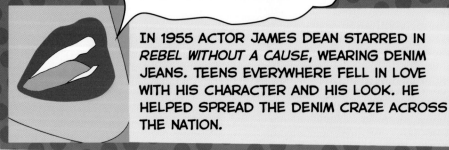

Did You Know ?

IN 1955 ACTOR JAMES DEAN STARRED IN *REBEL WITHOUT A CAUSE,* WEARING DENIM JEANS. TEENS EVERYWHERE FELL IN LOVE WITH HIS CHARACTER AND HIS LOOK. HE HELPED SPREAD THE DENIM CRAZE ACROSS THE NATION.

Traditional male clothing became fair game for both genders.

In 1984 a TV show called *Miami Vice* captured America's attention. Stars Don Johnson and Philip Michael Thomas created a sensation in men's wear. They wore brightly colored T-shirts under shiny suit jackets. Suddenly, men all over the country *had* to have these flashy clothes.

Fashion and Music

Musicians have played a huge part in sparking fashion trends. Elvis Presley had a great sense of personal style. When his music was first becoming popular in the 1950s, Elvis dressed conservatively—but with flair. He wore

Millions of young American men wanted to copy Elvis's rockin' style in the 1950s.

Avril Lavigne's fun, funky look is a hit with teens across America.

fashionable suits to show off his dance moves. During the 1960s Elvis began adding flamboyant scarves to his outfits. By the 1970s Elvis was wearing *truly* outrageous clothes. He performed in white jumpsuits that sparkled with rhinestones. Elvis's fans *loved* the outfits—it was all part of the show. Many fans tried to copy his special look.

Male musicians of the 1960s and 1970s performed glam rock. They wore wild outfits and makeup during their stage performances. David Bowie dyed his hair orange and wore skintight satin jumpsuits. Elton John wore platform shoes, feather boas, and glitter. Audiences loved—and imitated—it all.

Madonna's early fashion choices in the 1980s created a huge demand for fingerless gloves, black rubber bracelets, and net tank tops. Young girls across the country began to look like miniature copies of Madonna, imitating every fashion move she made.

When Nirvana became popular in the 1990s, their grunge look of flannel shirts, and ripped sweaters and jeans was adopted by teens across the nation. More recently, Avril Lavigne has become famous for wearing a tie, inspiring many of her fans to follow in her footsteps.

Some recent pop stars have taken this to a new level.

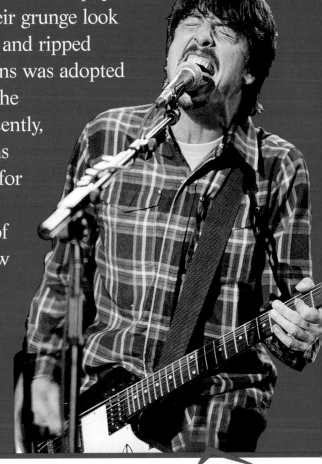

Dave Grohl and his Nirvana bandmates helped spread the Seattle-based grunge look from coast to coast.

Actress-turned-singer Jennifer Lopez actually started marketing her own fashions to her fans. She has a complete line of clothing for young women, featuring the "J Lo" label. Fans don't have to figure out ways to copy Lopez's look—they can buy it straight from the superstar's collection.

Always on the cutting edge of style, Jennifer Lopez inspires a new generation of fashion trends.

Russel Simmons, a hip-hop record producer, started his popular clothing line in 1992. Called Phat Farm, the company is based on the idea that hip-hop is not only a type of music, but also a way of life. Simmons created a line of men's sportswear, shoes, and accessories that capture this urban style. It included baggy pants, oversized athletic jerseys, and expensive sneakers. The clothing line became extremely successful. Several years later, his wife, Kimora Lee, added a women's line, Baby Phat, to the collection.

Fashion and First Ladies

First Lady Jacqueline Bouvier Kennedy was only thirty-one years old when she moved into the White House in 1961. She had a wonderful sense of style. American women were interested in her youthful approach to fashion. Clothing manufacturers created copies of Kennedy's elegant outfits for other women in the country.

From the moment she stepped into the spotlight in 1980, First Lady Nancy Reagan's taste in fashion was watched closely. Reagan's outfits were conservative. They were also stylish and often colorful. Reagan happily supported high-end American designers including Bill Blass and James Galanos. Reagan was considered a trendsetter among those who could afford her tastes in clothing, although most of what she wore was too expensive for the average American woman.

Jacqueline Kennedy influenced American fashion with her elegant, graceful look.

Fashion and Sports

Since the 1990s, sports have greatly influenced everyday American fashions. As interest in physical fitness has grown, so has the desire to highlight a well-toned body with sportswear. This trend fit in so well with America's casual look that sportswear became mainstream fashion.

Athletic wear has also brought about the use of new fabrics. Materials such as Gore-Tex® that help maintain body temperature were once used only for mountain-climbing and skiing gear. Now these materials are used in pants and coats for more casual use. Sports-team jerseys, jackets, and baseball caps have also found their way into everyday wear.

Sneakers, once worn only by athletes, are now an essential part of everyday American fashion. Sneakers have been around since the early 1900s, but took a major turn in 1958. Phil Knight, a student and track-runner at the University of Oregon, was unhappy with his uncomfortable, clumsy running shoes. Knight and his coach, Bill Bowerman, developed a lighter, more comfortable sneaker. It was a great

Superstar athlete Sarah Hughes always looks great on the ice. In 2002, she skated her way to an Olympic gold medal in a costume by designer Jeff Billings.

success. They went on to form the sneaker company that became Nike, Inc. The new sneaker became popular in sports *and* mainstream American fashion. The casual, comfortable shoe fit right in with America's popular look.

Celebrities play a large part in the connection between fashion and sports. Well-dressed athletes such as Tiger Woods and Serena Williams appear on advertisements for sportswear. Support from famous athletes can mean big money for a clothing designer. Sports figures have also used fashion design in their performances. Ice-skating champs Michelle Kwan and Sarah Hughes often wear outfits created by American designers. One of those designers, Vera Wang, was even a figure skater herself.

Is the future of fashion "phat"? Designer Kimora Lee Simmons and her daughter sure hope it is!

A Fashionable Future

Fashion is always changing. Often, by the time a trend is identified, new ones have taken its place. The future of fashion will depend on the future of the United States. As values and beliefs change, fashions will as well.

New Directions

Technology is forever evolving, and updates play a part in the fashion world. Modern technology allows fabrics to be made into clothing more quickly and easily. The Internet provides people with quick and easy access to the fashion scene both in America and in other countries. People can order clothing online, choosing popular styles and sizes with the help of virtual models on their computer screens.

Designers are finding inspiration in new places as well. Street fashions and vintage clothing were once thought of as unstylish. Now, more and more, these looks are making their way into America's mainstream designs. Fabric choices are changing as well. Many designers are embracing more natural materials, which could have an effect on their designs.

Passion From Parsons

Several of today's most exciting young designers are graduates of the Parsons School of Design in New York City. Among them is Robert Best, who worked for four years as a design assistant to the honored designer Isaac Mizrahi. Best also spent time as a designer of clothes for one of the most famous fashion models in the world—the Barbie doll! Now he designs collections for real women. His 2003 collection featured upscale cocktail party dresses that reminded many people of the 1950s and 1960s styles.

Other recent Parsons graduates include Jack McCollough and Lazaro Hernandez. Their design company Proenza Schouler, named after their mothers, showed their first design collection in 2003. It included classy evening wear and beautiful overcoats.

A Smaller World

More and more, independent designers are finding success with smaller shops. In many American cities, small-scale designers are opening their own boutiques in which to sell their designs. They even use these stores as workspaces to make clothing for customers.

A boutique allows designers to have the satisfaction of selling their own brand of clothing.

Did You Know ?

PARSONS SCHOOL OF DESIGN IS NOT THE ONLY PLACE TO STUDY FASHION IN NEW YORK STATE. THERE ARE MORE THAN TEN DIFFERENT SCHOOLS OFFERING PROGRAMS IN FASHION DESIGN. NO WONDER NEW YORK IS ONE OF THE FASHION CAPITALS OF THE WORLD!

Thousands of fashion students have dreams of being the next big designer to dress America.

These shops take quite a bit of time and money to run. Some designers who operate their own boutiques may still find department stores to carry their designs as well. This provides extra income to help with their private shops. Major department stores such as Barneys and Bloomingdale's sell many independent designers' styles.

People who buy clothes from independent designers often become loyal customers.

A FASHIONABLE FUTURE

It's fun to wear clothing that few other people have been seen wearing. Collecting pieces made by one designer is similar to collecting pieces of art by one artist. Boutiques allow a customer to develop a relationship with the designer.

Shopping for such one-of-a-kind clothing isn't cheap. However, there is great satisfaction in owning something unique. An executive at Henri Bendel, a department store in New York that features independent designers, told *Time* magazine, "Smaller brands have an emotional reach to the customer."

No one knows for sure what the future of fashion will be for America. Designers are constantly on the lookout for new styles, and people are eager to embrace new trends. Pop culture will always change, inspiring new ideas in years to come—and with so many talented up-and-coming designers, Americans can be sure they will certainly look their best!

new words

boutique (boo-**teek**) a small shop that sells fashionable clothes or other specialty items

canvas (**kan**-vuhss) a type of coarse, strong cloth used for tents, sails, and clothing

celebrity (suh-**leb**-ruh-tee) a famous person, especially an entertainer or movie star

chaperone (**shap**-uh-rohn) an adult who protects the safety of young people at an event such as a dance or class trip and who makes sure they behave well

conservative (kuhn-**sur**-vuh-tiv) moderate, cautious, and not extreme

denim (**den**-im) strong cotton material used to make jeans and other articles of clothing

elegant (**el**-uh-guhnt) graceful and stylish

embroidery (em-**broi**-dur-ee) a picture or design sewn onto cloth

essential (i-**sen**-shuhl) vital and important

flamboyant (flam-**boi**-uhnt) bold, showy, or brightly colored

identical (eye-**den**-ti-kuhl) exactly alike

New words

linen (**lin**-uhn) cloth made from the flax plant

mass-produced (**mass** pruh-**doosed**) made in large quantities by people or machines on an assembly line

paisley (**payz**-lee) marked with a swirled pattern of abstract, curved shapes

polyester (pol-ee-**ess**-tur) a synthetic substance used to make plastic products and fabric

retail (**ree**-tayl) having to do with the sale of goods directly to customers

silk (**silk**) a soft, shiny fabric made from fibers produced by a silkworm

sophisticated (suh-**fiss**-tuh-kay-tid) having a lot of knowledge about the world

velvet (**vel**-vit) a soft, thick fabric made from cotton, silk, or other materials

vintage (**vin**-tij) describing an earlier period in which something was made

virtual (**vir**-choo-uhl) something that looks three-dimensional and is created through a computer

FOR FURTHER READING

Bolino, Monika. *Fashion.* Farmington Hills: Gale Group, 2002.

Drill, Esther, Rebecca Odes, and Heather McDonald. *The Looks Book: A Whole New Approach to Beauty, Body, Image, and Style.* New York: Penguin Group, 2002.

Giacobello, John. *Choosing a Career in the Fashion Industry.* New York: Rosen Publishing, 2000.

Maze, Stephanie. *I Want to Be a Fashion Designer.* New York: Harcourt Children's Books, 2000.

Watson, Linda. *20th Century Fashion.* New York: Chelsea House Publishers, 2000.

Resources

Web Sites

Style.com: The Online Home of
Vogue and W
www.style.com
This is the official Web site of Vogue and W
magazines, featuring links to individual
designers, models, and fashion events.

Your Future in Fashion
www.thehighschoolgraduate.com/editorial/
USfashion.htm
Check out this informative Web site to learn
about what it takes to make it in the fashion
industry.

Teen Scene
http://fashion.about.com/blteenscene.htm
This fun site is updated each season with
information on the latest teen fashion trends.
Find promwear, read articles, and take the
teen fashion quiz.

Resources

Fashion Net

www.fashion.net

This site features fashion news updates from all over the world, and much more!

Fashion Design Colleges in the U.S.

www.justcolleges.com/us/us_fashion.phtml

Is fashion in your future? Visit this site for a list of fashion design college programs in the United States.

A Century of Fashion

www.factmonster.com/ipka/A0878570.html

Check out this site for a decade-by-decade look at fashion in the United States.

Index

InDex

About the Author
Ursula Rivera has been interested in fashion since she was a young child. Ursula grew up to be a writer and has written titles on popular culture and American celebrities.